More Than Rubies

A Modern Woman's Guide to Living with Purpose, Virtue, & Strength

By Daphne Nicole Mace

More Than Rubies: A Modern Woman's Guide to Living with Purpose, Virtue & Strength

ISBN: 9798316691791

Printed in the United States of America

Published by: Daphne Nicole Mace

Cover and interior design by Daphne Nicole Mace

Dedication

To My Mother and Grandmothers -
Thank you for being examples of strength,
grace, and unconditional love.
Your prayers, sacrifices, and wisdom have
shaped the woman I am today.
This book reflects the legacy you've
poured into me.

And to every woman holding these pages
in her hands -
Keep going. Keep growing. Keep
becoming.
You are more than rubies.

For every woman struggling to know her
worth -
You are more than enough.
You are more than rubies.

Table of Contents

Introduction

The Modern Struggle vs. Biblical Virtue

We live in a world that's constantly trying to define us. It tells us we must be *strong but soft, independent but nurturing, confident but not "too much."* We scroll through highlight reels on social media, compare our behind-the-scenes to someone else's filtered life, and wonder if we're falling behind. We chase careers, relationships, validation, and sometimes even peace—only to find ourselves tired, confused, or questioning who we really are.

Somewhere in the noise, the woman God created us to be gets lost.

But what if the answer isn't in becoming *who the world wants*, but becoming *who God designed*?

That's what led me here. That's what brought you here. And that's what this book is all about.

Why the Proverbs 31 Woman Still Matters

For years, I avoided Proverbs 31. I thought she was perfect—too perfect. She ran businesses, took care of her household, gave to the poor, honored her husband, raised children, and feared the Lord. I thought, *"Whew, that's not me. I can barely keep my room clean and get my prayer life in order."*

But then God showed me something. The Proverbs 31 woman is not a checklist. She's not a Pinterest-worthy standard to stress over. She's a blueprint. A reflection of what happens when a woman walks in purpose, leans into God's wisdom, and lives with intention.

She is powerful because of her *character*, not her calendar. She's not praised because she does it all—she's praised because she does what *matters*, and she does it with virtue and strength.

In today's world, we need women like her more than ever—women who build, nurture, lead, and love from a place of wholeness. We need women who fear the Lord more than they fear failure. We need women who rise in strength and rest in grace.

What "Becoming Her" Really Means

Becoming a Proverbs 31 woman isn't about *doing more*—it's about *becoming more* of who you already are in Christ. It's about transformation from the inside out. It's a journey—not toward perfection, but toward purpose.

In these pages, I'm not here to give you another religious to-do list. I'm here to walk with you. We'll go verse by verse, principle by principle, and bring each one into our modern lives with clarity, honesty, and love.

You'll find reflections, prayers, and real conversations about identity, womanhood, purpose, marriage, business, health, and legacy. Whether you're single, married, starting over, or still finding your footing—you belong here. You are becoming her. Day by day, choice by choice, moment by moment.

You are *More Than Rubies*.

Let's begin.

Chapter 1: More Precious Than Rubies

"Who can find a virtuous woman? For her price is far above rubies." — Proverbs 31:10

Understanding Your Worth

Let's be honest—most of us have spent *some part* of our lives questioning our worth.

We've let it be shaped by the opinions of others, our past mistakes, our relationship status, our productivity, or even our bank account. Some days we feel worthy, other days we feel invisible. But here's what Proverbs 31:10 tells us—*our value is not based on what we do, but on who we are.*

The Bible says a virtuous woman's worth is *far above rubies.* Not just *equal* to rubies... *above* them. Rubies are rare, beautiful, and incredibly valuable—but a woman of virtue? She's *more*.

That means you are more than your shame.
More than your trauma.
More than your Instagram feed.
More than your past.
More than what they said.

You are a **daughter of the King**, and that makes you royalty. Not because of perfection, but because of identity.

Letting Go of False Labels

The enemy's favorite tactic is to lie to us about who we are. If he can keep you believing you're not good enough, you'll never step into who God called you to be.

Maybe you've been labeled as too emotional, too independent, too broken, too quiet, too loud, too much, or not enough.

But God never called you any of those things. He calls you *fearfully and*

wonderfully made.
He calls you *chosen.*
He calls you *redeemed.*
He calls you *His.*

This journey is not just about *becoming her*—it's about *remembering who you've always been* in God's eyes.

Virtue Is Not Perfection

Now let's clear something up: being "virtuous" doesn't mean being perfect. Virtue in Hebrew (chayil) actually means **strength, ability, excellence, and valor**—it's a word often used to describe warriors!

So when God says your worth is far above rubies, He's not saying you have to be flawless. He's saying your *character* is powerful. Your *heart* is valuable. Your *strength*, your *compassion*, your *integrity*—they all matter.

Virtue means choosing to honor God even when no one is watching. It means showing up in love, grace, truth, and courage. It means being both soft and strong.

And guess what? That version of you already exists inside of you. She's not far away—she's waiting for permission to rise.

Let's Reflect

1. In what areas of your life have you struggled to believe you're valuable?

2. What false labels or lies do you need to let go of?

3. How can you begin to walk in your true identity this week?

Prayer

Father, thank You for creating me with intention and purpose. Thank You that my worth isn't found in the world but in You. Help me to release every false label and lie that has kept me stuck. Remind me daily that I am more than rubies. Make me a woman of virtue, strength, and unwavering faith. In Jesus' name, amen.

Affirmation

I am more than rubies.
I am chosen. I am strong. I am virtuous.
I am who God says I am.

Chapter 2: Trustworthy and True

"The heart of her husband safely trusts in her, so that he shall have no lack of gain."
— Proverbs 31:11

Being a Safe Space

Whether you're single, dating, or married—this verse hits deep. Why? Because it's not just about being a "good wife." It's about being a *safe woman.*

The Proverbs 31 woman is someone whose heart, words, actions, and presence bring **stability**, not chaos. She can be trusted—with emotions, with money, with plans, with people. She's not reckless with what's been entrusted to her. She carries herself with grace and responsibility.

Let's be real—being trustworthy is not just about *what* you do; it's about *who* you are when no one's watching.

Can You Be Trusted?

Let's flip the script for a second and get honest:
Can God trust you?
Can others trust you?
Can you even trust yourself?

Do your words match your actions?
Do you keep confidences or do you gossip "in prayer"?
Do you show up when it's inconvenient?
Do you honor your commitments—even the ones you made to *yourself*?

Trust isn't just about relationships with others—it's a cornerstone of your relationship with God, and with yourself. God wants to entrust you with purpose, with blessings, with people, and yes— even with love and marriage. But before He releases the promise, He checks for **character**.

Emotional Integrity

The heart of her husband safely trusts in her.

That phrase "safely trust" carries weight. It speaks to emotional security. It means she's not manipulative. She doesn't weaponize his vulnerability or use his flaws against him.

And sis—even if you're not married yet, this is the time to build that muscle.

Emotional integrity looks like:

- Not needing to "win" every argument

- Knowing how to listen without interrupting

- Having honest conversations without tearing someone down

- Being the kind of woman who doesn't *trigger*, she *heals*

That's the Proverbs 31 kind of trust. The kind that brings peace, not pressure.

Building Trust Takes Time

Let's be real: trust doesn't just appear—it's built. Layer by layer. Moment by moment. And it can also be lost. That's why it's so important to be consistent in both public and private.

Start small:

- Keep your promises—even to yourself.

- Guard what others share with you.

- Show up on time.

- Do what you said you would do.

Trust is built in the *little things.* And that trust becomes the foundation for relationships that are strong, healthy, and honoring to God.

Let's Reflect

1. In what areas of your life are you consistent and trustworthy?

2. Where do you need to grow in emotional integrity?

3. What does it look like to be a safe space for others (friends, family, future spouse)?

Prayer

Lord, grow me into a woman who can be trusted. Teach me how to be faithful in the small things and consistent in my character. Help me to speak with love, act with integrity, and be a safe space for the people You've placed in my life. I want to reflect Your faithfulness in everything I do. In Jesus' name, amen.

Affirmation

I am a woman of integrity.
I am trustworthy.
I am a safe space.
I reflect God's faithfulness in every area of my life.

Chapter 3: Doing Good, Not Harm

"She does him good and not harm all the days of her life." — Proverbs 31:12

Intentional Goodness

The Proverbs 31 woman *chooses* to do good. Not just when she feels like it. Not just when it's easy. The verse says she does him good **all the days of her life**— meaning she's consistent, intentional, and faithful in how she shows up.

Let's sit with that for a minute.

Doing good isn't passive. It's not "just being nice." It's an **active choice** to uplift, support, encourage, and protect the people in your life—especially the ones God has called you to love intimately.

But here's the key: this doesn't start with marriage. This starts with *you*.

Before you're someone's wife, mother, or partner—you're God's daughter. And He's asking: **Are you someone who brings good wherever you go?**

The Power of Presence

Sometimes doing good is about **what you say.**
Other times, it's about **what you choose not to say.**

Sometimes it's helping with tasks.
Other times it's just being present when someone needs a quiet moment or a safe hug.

Doing good might mean:

- Praying for someone even when they don't ask

- Encouraging a friend when you're tired yourself

- Choosing not to bring up their past when you're angry

- Speaking truth with grace, not guilt

And yes—it might also mean being kind to yourself, forgiving yourself, and learning to treat yourself the way God treats you.

Breaking the Habit of Harm

Let's be real. Harm doesn't always look like big betrayal or abuse. Sometimes it's the subtle stuff that erodes trust and love over time:

- Sarcasm that cuts too deep

- Silent treatment that punishes

- Complaining instead of communicating

- Criticizing instead of covering in prayer

We've all been there. But growing into the woman God called you to be means confronting those tendencies head-on and asking, *"Am I doing good—or harm?"*

And if you've caused harm in the past—hear this: *There is grace for that.* God's not looking for perfect women. He's looking for **willing** ones.

Goodness is a Lifestyle

When you become a woman who does good and not harm, it doesn't just bless your future husband—it blesses your family, your friendships, your workplace, your church, and your business.

It becomes a lifestyle.
A signature.
Your divine fingerprint.

And when you live like that, you're not just becoming a Proverbs 31 woman... you're becoming a light in a dark world.

Let's Reflect

1. Think of a time you chose to do good—even when it was hard. How did it impact you or others?

2. Are there any habits, attitudes, or patterns that could be causing harm (even unintentionally)?

3. How can you intentionally do good this week—in your words, actions, and presence?

Prayer

Father, create in me a heart that desires to do good. Help me to recognize the power of my words, actions, and presence. I don't want to just be good to those I love—I want to reflect *Your* goodness in everything I do. Show me how to build others up, protect their hearts, and love well. In Jesus' name, amen.

Affirmation

I do good and not harm.
I am a builder, not a breaker.
I reflect God's goodness in all I do.

Chapter 4: Willing Hands & Hustle

"She seeks wool and flax, and works with willing hands." — Proverbs 31:13

She Works... Willingly

There's something so powerful about the phrase **"willing hands."** It tells us that the Proverbs 31 woman doesn't just work—she works with *heart.*

She doesn't move out of bitterness, burnout, or obligation. She doesn't resent the work God has given her. Instead, she works with *willingness*—an open heart, a willing spirit, and a mindset that honors her assignment.

Let's be honest: sometimes we want the results without the responsibility. The dream without the discipline. The fruit without the faithfulness.

But the woman God celebrates? She *shows up.* Not just for others—but for the call on her life.

The Myth of "Effortless"

We're living in a culture obsessed with **"soft life" energy**—and listen, I'm all for peace, ease, and rest. But let's not confuse that with *laziness in the name of self-care.*

Being a Proverbs 31 woman doesn't mean hustling in your own strength—but it *does* mean putting your hands to what God has given you. She isn't afraid to **grind with grace.** To build something. To stay committed. To finish what she starts.

Because the truth is: purpose requires participation.

The work she does isn't just about money. It's about meaning. It's about building something with her life that matters.

Your Hands Are Holy

The Proverbs 31 woman sought wool and flax—materials used to make garments for her household and goods to sell. That means she was **intentional** about what she pursued. She didn't chase distractions—she went after resources that served her calling.

Ask yourself:

- What are you reaching for with your hands?

- Are you building something that glorifies God—or just surviving the day?

- Are your hands busy or are they fruitful?

When your hands are surrendered to God, **ordinary tasks become holy acts.** Laundry becomes service. Crafting becomes ministry. Business becomes a tool for legacy. Raising children becomes kingdom work.

Don't Wait for Motivation—Choose Discipline

Willing hands don't mean you're *always in the mood.* Let's keep it real—motivation fades. But **discipline is a decision.** It's what you do when the feeling is gone, but the assignment still matters.

If God has called you to it—whether that's school, motherhood, business, ministry, or healing—show up for it. Put your hands to it with faith and intention. Not just out of duty, but out of love.

You don't need to do it perfectly.
You just need to do it *willingly.*

Let's Reflect

1. What has God placed in your hands right now—business, family, gifts, dreams?

2. Are you approaching your work with willingness or weariness?

3. What distractions do you need to remove so your hands can stay focused on what matters?

Prayer

Lord, give me willing hands and a willing heart. Help me to work with joy, not just obligation. Teach me how to honor the work You've given me—whether it's building, serving, creating, or resting. I want to show up for my purpose with consistency, excellence, and grace. Use my hands for Your glory. In Jesus' name, amen.

Affirmation

My hands are willing.
My work has meaning.
I show up with purpose, not pressure.
God is using what's in my hands to build something eternal.

"She considers a field and buys it; with the fruit of her hands she plants a vineyard." — Proverbs 31:16

Sis Was a Businesswoman. Period.

Let's just pause and appreciate this:
She **considered a field**—meaning she used *wisdom* and *discernment*.
She **bought it**—meaning she took *action* and *made investments*.
She **planted a vineyard**—meaning she *cultivated* something that would produce income, legacy, and nourishment.

That's not a passive woman.
That's not a woman waiting around to be rescued.
That's a **purpose-driven, business-minded, bold woman** of God.

She wasn't just praying—she was producing.

She wasn't just hoping—she was harvesting.

That same spirit is in you.

Faith & Finances Go Together

For too long, some of us have been made to feel like wanting success, running a business, or earning money is somehow "unspiritual." But *God is a multiplier*. He honors stewardship, vision, strategy, and bold faith.

The Proverbs 31 woman didn't just make money—she **built wealth**.
She didn't just make sales—she **created systems**.
She didn't just spend—she **invested**.

And she did it while still honoring her family, her values, and her God. That's the balance we strive for.

You don't have to choose between business and godliness.
You can do **both**—with boldness, excellence, and integrity.

Use What's in Your Hands

You don't need a six-figure bank account to get started. You just need a **willing heart** and a vision from God. The Proverbs 31 woman used what she had—her hands, her resources, her wisdom—and turned it into something lasting.

So what's in *your* hands?

- A creative gift?

- A business idea?

- A side hustle?

- A passion to serve others?

Don't sit on it. Pray over it. Plan it out. Launch it. God can't bless what you refuse to build.

You Can Be Bold AND Humble

Boldness doesn't mean arrogance. It means **confidence in the God who called you.** You can walk into boardrooms, boutiques, pop-up shops, or online platforms knowing that your business isn't just about profit—it's about purpose.

You're not just selling products.
You're creating solutions.
You're solving problems.
You're carrying influence.
You're shifting atmospheres.

God's favor on your hands is your secret sauce.

Let's Reflect

1. What gifts, talents, or business ideas has God placed inside of you?

2. What fears or limiting beliefs are holding you back from stepping into bold action?

3. What would it look like to start or scale something in faith this year?

Prayer

Lord, thank You for the vision and creativity You've placed in me. Help me to be bold and wise, to plan with purpose and move with faith. I surrender my gifts, my goals, and my business ideas to You. Teach me how to steward them well—not for applause, but for Your glory. In Jesus' name, amen.

Affirmation

I am business-minded and bold.
God has gifted me to build, grow, and multiply.
I create with purpose, lead with faith, and walk in wisdom.
My hands are blessed. My work is holy.

"She rises while it is yet night and provides food for her household and portions for her maidens." — Proverbs 31:15

She Doesn't Just Wake Up—She Rises

There's a difference between *getting up* and *rising.*

Getting up is routine. Rising is intentional. It means showing up early, with purpose, even when no one sees or claps for it. The Proverbs 31 woman didn't just wake up and wing it—she rose **with direction**.

Let's be honest—modern life is filled with distractions. It's easy to spend the first moments of the day scrolling, stressing, or snoozing. But this woman models something different: she starts her day in a posture of **service, strategy, and stewardship.**

This doesn't mean you need to become a 5AM miracle morning girl overnight—but it *does* mean starting your day **on purpose**.

Productivity Is More Than Doing

We live in a culture that glorifies "busy." But busy doesn't always mean fruitful.

The Proverbs 31 woman isn't praised for being exhausted—she's honored for being *effective*. She's prepared. She knows what her people need, and she makes moves to meet those needs with love and grace.

Preparation is a form of love.
It says, "I thought ahead."
It says, "I care enough to be intentional."
It says, "I'm not reacting—I'm leading."

Being prepared might look like:

- Planning your meals or workweek in advance

- Laying out clothes the night before

- Setting aside time to pray, journal, and hear from God

- Delegating tasks so you don't drown in them

Preparedness frees you from chaos—and gives you space to *live fully*.

Don't Confuse Rest with Laziness

Yes, the Proverbs 31 woman rose early— but don't get it twisted—she also lived in **balance**. She didn't neglect her well-being just to serve others. Productivity, in God's Kingdom, includes *rest, Sabbath, and rhythms of grace.*

You can prepare and still take breaks. You can plan ahead and still have peace. You can get things done without running yourself into the ground.

True productivity isn't about how *much* you do—it's about doing what actually *matters.*

Your Season Requires Strategy

Every season of life has different demands. Whether you're:

- A college student,

- A mom of toddlers,

- A working woman,

- An entrepreneur,

- Or somewhere in between...

God wants to help you create *structure* and *flow* that aligns with your purpose. What works for someone else might not be your rhythm—and that's okay. Your job isn't to copy. Your job is to *clarify* and *commit.*

Ask God: "What do *my people* need? What does *this season* require of me?" Then plan accordingly.

Let's Reflect

1. What's one area of your life that feels chaotic or unstructured?

2. What simple morning or evening routine could help you feel more prepared?

3. How can you be more intentional with your time without burning out?

Prayer

Father, thank You for being a God of order and peace. Teach me how to prepare with grace and purpose. Help me to rise with intention, to serve those around me, and to manage my time in a way that honors You. I give You my schedule, my energy, and my tasks—make them fruitful. In Jesus' name, amen.

Affirmation

I rise with purpose.
I prepare in love.
I am productive, not just busy.
God orders my days and gives me strength for every assignment.

"She opens her hand to the poor and reaches out her hands to the needy." — Proverbs 31:20

Compassion Is Her Character

A virtuous woman isn't just smart and strong—she's *soft-hearted, too.*

She doesn't just focus on her own goals or her own household—she **looks outward**. She sees the needs of others and responds with compassion, not judgment. She doesn't just give from her overflow; she gives from her heart.

Generosity is not a personality trait—it's a **spiritual posture.** And the Proverbs 31 woman lives with *open hands.*

We're Called to Care

This verse isn't just a feel-good idea—it's a *command.* As daughters of the King, we are *called* to care for the poor, the overlooked, the broken, the lonely, and the marginalized.

That doesn't always mean financial giving. Sometimes your generosity looks like:

- A kind word

- A shared resource

- Helping someone with no expectation in return

- Giving time, presence, or prayer

To "open your hand" means you're not clinging to what you have—it means you trust God as your source and *you're willing to be a vessel*.

Don't Wait to Have More

One of the biggest lies the enemy tells us is: *"Once you have more, then you'll give."*

But real generosity isn't about how much you have—it's about how much you're *willing to release*.

If you only have $10 but you give $1 with love and obedience—that's *blessed.* If you only have a few hours a week, but you use one to encourage someone or volunteer—that *matters.*

God blesses *willing hearts*, not wealthy pockets.

The Reach of Her Hands

This verse says she "reaches out her hands to the needy." In other words, she doesn't wait for people to come to her—she *goes to them.*

This is a woman who takes **action.** She sees a need, and instead of saying, *"That's not my business,"* she says, *"How can I serve?"*

This is ministry.
This is Kingdom work.
This is the Gospel in motion.

And it doesn't always happen in a church building—it happens in DMs, grocery stores, sidewalks, lunchrooms, and coffee shop conversations.

You Are a Blessing on Assignment

You were not placed on this earth to simply exist or collect blessings. You were created to be a **conduit of blessing.**

God wants to flow *through* you.
Your time. Your story. Your healing. Your finances. Your platform. Your business. It's all Kingdom currency.

The Proverbs 31 woman shows us what it looks like to live in such a way that others are lifted because of her obedience.

Let's Reflect

1. Who in your life (or community) could use encouragement, support, or love right now?

2. What excuses or fears have kept you from giving, serving, or helping?

3. What's one way you can open your
   hands this week—big or small?

Prayer

Lord, give me eyes to see the needs
around me and a heart that's willing to
respond. Help me to live with open hands
and trust You as my source. Use me to be
a blessing to others—through my time,
talents, and resources. I want to reflect
Your compassion and kindness in
everything I do. In Jesus' name, amen.

Affirmation

I live with open hands.
I give freely and serve joyfully.
I am a vessel of compassion.
God uses me to bless others.

Chapter 8: Clothed with Strength

*"She is clothed with strength and dignity;
she can laugh at the days to come."* —
Proverbs 31:25

This Strength Isn't Just Physical

When the Bible says she is "clothed with
strength," it's not just talking about her
muscles or her stamina. This strength is
layered. It's *emotional, mental, spiritual,*
and yes—*physical* too.

It's not the kind of strength that comes
from hustling 24/7.
It's the kind of strength that comes from
knowing who you are and *who your God is.*

This woman doesn't wear insecurity or
anxiety. She wears *dignity.*
She doesn't let fear dress her. She's
clothed in *courage.*
And because of that—she can *laugh at the
days to come.*

That kind of peace is a flex.

What Are You Clothed In?

Every day, we wake up and "put on" something—mentally, emotionally, spiritually.

Some of us wear:

- Fear

- Self-doubt

- Bitterness

- Stress

- Guilt

- Shame

But God is calling you to *strip those off* and be **clothed with strength and dignity.**

You weren't meant to carry every burden.
You weren't created to be in survival mode.
You were designed to be clothed in grace, boldness, wisdom, and faith.

What you wear spiritually *affects how you walk.*

Dignity is Divine Confidence

Let's talk about *dignity.*

Dignity doesn't mean pride or arrogance. It means you carry yourself with quiet confidence, knowing you belong to God.

It means you don't lower your standards for attention.
You don't shrink yourself for approval.
You don't entertain what drains you.

Dignity looks like:

- Knowing when to speak and when to be silent

- Walking away from things that don't honor your worth

- Loving yourself enough to heal

- Trusting God when others don't see your value

This woman doesn't chase validation—
she moves in identity.

She Laughs Without Fear

Now *this* is powerful: "She can laugh at
the days to come."

Why? Because she's not afraid of the
future.
She's not overwhelmed by uncertainty.
She's not shaken by what-ifs or worst-
case scenarios.

She has **faith** that God is already in her
tomorrow.
She trusts that even when life doesn't go
as planned—*His plan still prevails.*

Her joy isn't based on her circumstances.
It's rooted in the One who never changes.

That kind of peace? That kind of
confidence? That's the fruit of a life
anchored in God.

Let's Reflect

1. What have you been "wearing" emotionally or mentally that you need to take off?

2. What would it look like to walk clothed in strength and dignity?

3. What fears about the future are keeping you from resting and laughing in the present?

Prayer

Lord, help me to remove anything that doesn't reflect who You created me to be. Clothe me in Your strength. Wrap me in Your dignity. Let me walk with boldness, rooted in identity, and laugh without fear of the future. I trust that You are already in my tomorrow. In Jesus' name, amen.

Affirmation

I am clothed in strength.
I walk in dignity.
I do not fear the future—because God is

already there.
I laugh with joy, move with confidence,
and rest in grace.

Chapter 9: Honoring Her Husband

"Her husband is known in the gates, when he sits among the elders of the land." — Proverbs 31:23

A Wife Who Honors

This verse doesn't directly talk about what *she* is doing—yet her influence is unmistakable.

Her husband is known and respected in public spaces—**because of the kind of woman she is in private**.

Her honor lifts him. Her wisdom supports him. Her presence empowers him.

Now hear this: This doesn't mean her worth is tied to a man. The Proverbs 31 woman is *already whole*. But when she enters a marriage covenant, she doesn't compete—she *complements*. She doesn't overshadow—she *strengthens*.

That kind of partnership takes *maturity, humility,* and *grace.*

Power in Partnership

Marriage isn't about being someone's accessory—it's about being a **partner.**
A helpmate. A covering. A source of peace, wisdom, and strength.

When a woman walks in her identity and purpose, she naturally contributes to her husband's success—not just in career, but in character, in calling, and in confidence.

The Proverbs 31 woman's love *elevates* her husband.
She's not trying to be the man.
She's not trying to control him.
She honors him as he leads, and he honors her as his equal.

This is **mutual submission**, fueled by reverence for God.

Marriage Starts Before Marriage

Even if you're single right now, this chapter is for *you too*. Because the habits, mindsets, and spiritual maturity that make a godly wife **begin before the wedding**.

If you desire marriage, ask yourself:

- Am I creating peace or drama in my relationships?

- Do I communicate with love or with defensiveness?

- Do I pray for my future husband now—not just for who he is, but for who I'll be when I meet him?

Marriage isn't the goal—**ministry through marriage** is.
And that ministry starts with the way you live and love today.

Honor in a Culture of Disrespect

We live in a world that celebrates "clapbacks," sarcasm, and putting people in their place. But the Proverbs 31 woman isn't moved by culture—she's led by **kingdom character.**

She doesn't belittle her man in public.
She doesn't roll her eyes and make him the punchline.
She builds him up—because *a secure woman doesn't need to tear down.*

And the fruit? He's respected in the gates. His reputation reflects her strength, and hers reflects his.

That's honor in action. ☞

Let's Reflect

1. What does honor look like to you— in words, actions, and attitude?

2. How do you currently show honor to your spouse, or prepare to be a woman who honors her future husband?

3. Are there any areas in your relationships where God is calling

you to lead with more grace,
support, or humility?

Prayer

Father, teach me how to honor not just
with my words, but with my heart.
Whether I'm preparing for marriage or
already in it, help me to be a woman who
uplifts, encourages, and partners with
purpose. Remove pride, selfishness, and
fear—and replace them with humility,
wisdom, and grace. Let my love reflect
Your love. In Jesus' name, amen.

Affirmation

I am a woman who honors.
I speak life. I build trust. I lead with grace.
Whether single or married, I prepare my
heart for partnership.
My love brings peace, and my presence
brings strength.

Chapter 10: Managing Her Home

"She looks well to the ways of her household and does not eat the bread of idleness." — Proverbs 31:27

Her Home Reflects Her Heart

The Proverbs 31 woman doesn't just live in a house—she *creates a home.*

She "looks well to the ways of her household"—which means she's **aware**, **attentive**, and **intentional** about the atmosphere she's cultivating. Her home is not just clean—it's peaceful. It's not just decorated—it's sacred.

She understands that what happens behind closed doors matters just as much as what people see in public.

Order is Spiritual

Let's talk about it—**order is a form of love.** It's not about being a perfectionist or having an Instagram-worthy kitchen. It's about creating an environment where:

- You can think clearly

- Your family can rest peacefully

- Guests feel welcomed

- God's presence is honored

Clutter in your space can create clutter in your mind. The Proverbs 31 woman doesn't let disorder take over her space or her spirit. She makes room—for peace, productivity, and purpose.

Idleness vs. Rest

Now, don't miss this: the verse says she *"does not eat the bread of idleness."* That doesn't mean she never rests—it means she's not lazy or careless with her time.

There's a difference between **rest and idleness**:

- **Rest** is intentional. It's a reset. It's biblical.

- **Idleness** is avoidance. It's delay. It's rooted in distraction or discouragement.

The Proverbs 31 woman understands her rhythms. She works when it's time to work. She rests when it's time to rest. And she doesn't let procrastination become a lifestyle.

Stewardship Over Perfection

Managing your home well doesn't mean it's spotless 24/7. It means you're **stewarding what you've been given—** with care, with gratitude, and with vision.

Whether you live in a high-rise or a small room, whether it's just you or a full family, managing your home means:

- Taking responsibility

- Creating beauty and peace

- Protecting the spiritual atmosphere

- Building a space that aligns with your values

Your home should speak of who you are—and more importantly, *whose* you are.

Home is Ministry

Your home is your first ministry.
It's where your faith is practiced, your character is refined, and your love is tested.

The Proverbs 31 woman ministers to her household—not just through chores, but through her tone, her attitude, and her presence. She sets the standard—not out of control, but out of care.

Whether you're single or married, kids or no kids—ask yourself:
What kind of home am I building?
What does it feel like to live with me?

That's the real home management.

Let's Reflect

1. What kind of atmosphere are you creating in your home?

2. What does "looking well to the ways of your household" look like for you in this season?

3. Are there any areas of idleness or disorganization God is calling you to bring back into order?

Prayer

Lord, thank You for the space I call home. Teach me how to manage it with wisdom, peace, and grace. Help me create an atmosphere that honors You—a place where Your presence can dwell. Show me how to steward what You've given me well, and give me the strength to stay focused, faithful, and fruitful. In Jesus' name, amen.

Affirmation

My home is a sanctuary.
I manage it with wisdom, peace, and purpose.
I reject idleness and walk in stewardship.
My home reflects the heart of God.

Chapter 11: Wisdom on Her Tongue

"She opens her mouth with wisdom, and the teaching of kindness is on her tongue."
— Proverbs 31:26

The Way She Speaks Sets the Tone

Words are powerful.

And the Proverbs 31 woman doesn't use hers recklessly—she uses them to **teach, encourage, correct, guide, and protect**.

This woman *thinks before she speaks*. She doesn't use her tongue to gossip, curse, tear down, or wound. She knows that her voice carries weight—so she chooses **wisdom and kindness** every time she opens her mouth.

She doesn't just talk to be heard.
She speaks to help.
She speaks to heal.
She speaks with *purpose.*

Words That Build, Not Break

Let's be honest—most of us have said things we regret. Maybe it was in anger, fear, insecurity, or defense. But as we grow into Proverbs 31 women, God calls us to level up our **language**.

Ask yourself:

- Do my words bring peace or pressure?

- Do I build others up—or subtly tear them down?

- Do I speak truth with love—or with shame?

Kindness is not weakness. It's **strength under control.**
Wisdom is not silence. It's *knowing what to say, when to say it, and how to say it.*

She Teaches by Example

This verse says "the teaching of kindness is on her tongue"—which means she's not just kind in private, she **teaches others** how to be kind too—through her words, tone, and presence.

Whether it's kids, mentees, team members, or friends—*people learn from how you speak.*

So what are you teaching them?

Are you teaching them how to honor God in speech?
Are you teaching them how to handle conflict with grace?
Are you teaching them how to hold truth and kindness in the same sentence?

You don't need a platform to teach—your mouth is a ministry.

Silence is Sometimes the Wisest Response

Wisdom also knows *when not to speak.* Sometimes the most powerful thing you can do is **pause**.

When you're angry, tempted to clap back, or ready to drop a passive-aggressive "truth"... ask the Holy Spirit to help you pause and speak in love—or stay silent if it's not your battle.

Just because it's true doesn't mean it's timely.
Just because you feel it doesn't mean you have to say it.
The Proverbs 31 woman doesn't just react—she *responds*.

Let's Reflect

1. What patterns do you notice in your speech (tone, reactions, word choice)?

2. Who looks to you for guidance— whether as a mom, friend, sister, mentor, or leader?

3. What would it look like to open your mouth with wisdom and kindness in tough moments?

Prayer

Lord, tame my tongue. Fill my mouth with wisdom and kindness. Teach me how to speak words that heal, guide, and reflect Your character. Help me to pause before I speak, and let my words always align with Your will. I want to teach kindness, not just with my voice—but with my life. In Jesus' name, amen.

Affirmation

I speak with wisdom.
Kindness is on my tongue.
My words build, bless, and bring peace.
God uses my voice to teach, lead, and heal.

Chapter 12: Her Children Rise and Call Her Blessed

"Her children rise up and call her blessed; her husband also, and he praises her." — Proverbs 31:28

Legacy Over Likes

In a culture obsessed with followers, likes, and going viral, this verse reminds us of what *really* matters—**the people who live closest to us, the ones who see us unfiltered.**

The Proverbs 31 woman's legacy is not just built on what she does—**it's built on who she is.**
Her children and husband rise—not because she's perfect, but because her love is consistent. Her influence is felt. Her presence leaves a mark.

This is the kind of woman whose life speaks **long after her words stop.** That's legacy.

Being Blessed is More Than Being Loved

The word "blessed" in this verse is deeper than just being liked or appreciated. It means **to be admired, respected, honored.** It speaks of *spiritual fruit*—not just emotional attachment.

Her children don't just say "I love my mom." They rise up and say, *"She is a blessing. Her life impacted mine."*

That's what we're building:

- Lives that shift atmospheres.

- Homes that feel safe and sacred.

- Memories rooted in love, wisdom, and truth.

- A reputation that honors God and heals generations.

Your Influence Begins Now

Whether you have children now, hope to one day, or are a spiritual mother to others—your legacy is already being written.

You are:

- Teaching someone how to love through your example.

- Showing someone how to persevere through your prayers.

- Inspiring someone to heal through your honesty.

Don't underestimate the power of your presence.

Children don't remember every gift or chore—they remember **how you made them feel.**
They remember the way you showed up.
The prayers you prayed.
The forgiveness you extended.
The lessons you lived out loud.

Let Them Rise

"Her children rise up…"

That part always gets me.

Your life should cause people to rise—to be better, to dream bigger, to love deeper, to know Jesus more intimately. Your character should stir something in those around you.

You don't need a platform to be impactful. You don't need a stage to be seen. If you're faithful in the quiet, God will multiply your impact in ways you can't even imagine.

Let's Reflect

1. How do you want to be remembered by those closest to you?

2. What kind of emotional and spiritual legacy are you building right now?

3. Who in your life (biological or spiritual) is already rising because of your love, leadership, or prayers?

Prayer

Lord, help me to live a life that blesses others. Let my children, family, friends, and future generations rise and call me blessed—not because I'm perfect, but because I've loved well and honored You. Shape me into the kind of woman who leaves a legacy of faith, wisdom, peace, and love. In Jesus' name, amen.

Affirmation

My life is leaving a legacy.
Those who know me are better because of God in me.
I am a blessing to my family and to future generations.
I am called, I am chosen, and I am building something eternal.

Chapter 13: Charm Fades, but Fear of the Lord Endures

"Charm is deceptive, and beauty is fleeting; but a woman who fears the Lord is to be praised." — Proverbs 31:30

Pretty Isn't Enough

We live in a world that glorifies charm and beauty.
The perfect Instagram feed. The glow-up.
The soft life aesthetic.
But the Word reminds us clearly—**charm can deceive, and beauty doesn't last.**

That's not a dig at being beautiful or taking care of yourself (God created beauty!). But it is a **warning**: if all you have is charm and appearance, you're building your value on something that *won't last.*

The Proverbs 31 woman is praised—not because she's flawless or fashionable—

but because she **fears the Lord.** That's where her true beauty begins.

What Is the Fear of the Lord?

Let's clarify: this isn't about being *scared* of God—it's about having **deep reverence, awe, and respect** for who He is.

A woman who fears the Lord:

- Seeks Him first in all things
- Honors His Word even when it's uncomfortable
- Lives with humility, not pride
- Leans on His wisdom, not just her own
- Submits her life, goals, and identity to His will

Her beauty isn't just skin-deep—it's **spirit-deep.**

The Kind of Woman That Lasts

Charm may get attention.
Beauty may turn heads.
But **character sustains legacy.**

The Proverbs 31 woman doesn't just
want to be admired—she wants to be
remembered for her faith, her wisdom, her
love, and her obedience to God.

In a culture chasing trends, she's
anchored in **timeless truth.**

She's not trying to outshine other
women—she's walking in **divine light.**
She's not chasing validation—she's
walking in **God's approval.**

Your Spirit Is the Real Glow

The most radiant women are those who:

- Pray in secret

- Love without condition

- Forgive quickly

- Walk humbly

- And light up every room—not with their style, but with their *spirit.*

When you fear the Lord, you become a woman who is *praiseworthy* not just here on earth—but in Heaven.

You don't need to perform.
You don't need to prove.
You just need to *pursue* God.

Everything else flows from that.

Let's Reflect

1. Where have you felt pressure to rely on charm, beauty, or approval?

2. What does "fearing the Lord" look like in your daily life?

3. How can you build your confidence and identity on God's truth instead of the world's standards?

Prayer

Father, help me to live a life that honors
You above everything else. Let my heart
be anchored in truth, not trends. Teach
me to fear You—not with dread, but with
love, reverence, and awe. Make my beauty
come from the inside out. Let me be
known not just for how I look, but for how
I love, serve, and walk with You. In Jesus'
name, amen.

Affirmation

I fear the Lord, and that is my beauty.
I don't chase charm—I chase character.
I'm rooted in truth, clothed in strength,
and led by purpose.
I am becoming a woman who lasts.

Chapter 14: Give Her the Fruit of Her Hands

"Honor her for all that her hands have done, and let her works bring her praise at the city gate." — Proverbs 31:31 (NIV)

She Reaps What She Sowed

After all the verses describing her character, work, and heart—this one ends with what she receives: **honor, praise, and fruit.** ☐

Not because she went viral.
Not because she was loud.
But because she *faithfully built what God put in her hands.*

This verse is a **divine reminder** that when you show up in obedience, love, and purpose—**you will reap.**
Maybe not immediately. Maybe not in the way you expected. But God *sees everything.* And He's a rewarder of those who diligently seek Him.

You Deserve to Be Honored

Let's pause right here and say this: **you
are worthy of honor.**
Not for perfection.
Not for doing it all.
But for showing up, day after day, with a
willing heart.

This verse is not about pride—it's about
permission. Permission to celebrate the
woman who:

- Loved through pain

- Prayed through storms

- Built through burnout

- Stayed soft when life tried to make
  her hard

- Chose faith when it would've been
  easier to quit

God says: *"Let her be praised."*

You're Walking Into Harvest

The fruit of your hands could look like:

- Peace in your home

- Restoration in your marriage

- A thriving business

- A healed heart

- A deeper relationship with God

- Children who carry your wisdom

- A testimony that sets others free

This isn't just about success—it's about **spiritual legacy.**

Everything you've planted in love, obedience, and faith—**God is going to honor it.**

You are not overlooked. You are not behind. You are *becoming.* And what's ahead is *worth it.*

Let's Reflect

1. What have you faithfully sown in this season—spiritually, emotionally, or practically?

2. Are you able to receive honor, or do you downplay what you've built?

3. How can you celebrate your growth without guilt?

Prayer

Lord, thank You for every seed I've planted in faith. Thank You for honoring my obedience, even when it felt hidden. Help me to walk boldly in the fruit of my hands. Teach me how to receive honor with humility and grace. Let my life reflect Your goodness and point back to You. In Jesus' name, amen.

Affirmation

I am worthy of honor.
I have sown in faith, and I will reap in joy.
My work is seen by Heaven and

celebrated in love.
I am walking in harvest season.

Chapter 15: Becoming Her in Singleness

Your Becoming Starts Now

If you're single, I want to tell you this loud and clear: **you don't have to wait for marriage to become a Proverbs 31 woman.**

You don't become *her* when you get a ring.
You don't become *her* when someone finally sees your worth.
You become *her* the moment you say, *"God, use me now."*

Singleness is not a punishment—it's preparation.
It's purpose.
It's a sacred space where God shapes your identity, heals your heart, and develops your strength.

You're Not Missing Anything

The enemy will try to convince you that you're behind, overlooked, or forgotten. But you're not "waiting" to be chosen—you've already been **called**.

This is your time to:

- Build your business

- Deepen your walk with God

- Heal your childhood wounds

- Travel, explore, and create

- Learn how to love yourself well

- Create habits that bless your future family

You're not just preparing for a husband. You're becoming a whole woman—for *you* and for *God.*

A Wife Before the Wedding

The Proverbs 31 woman was already operating as a wife before marriage was even mentioned. She was faithful, focused, wise, and spiritually mature. That's what *attracted* her husband's trust—not just her looks.

So, if you desire marriage, here's the secret:
Become the kind of woman who's so rooted in her purpose that her future husband *meets her in the field*, not in the DMs. ⩵

God Sees You

God hasn't forgotten your desire for love. But He loves you too much to rush the process. He's protecting you, preparing you, and positioning you for something *worth the wait.*

Don't lower your standards to speed up your timeline.
Don't shrink yourself to feel chosen.
Don't idolize marriage and miss the power of this season.

You are already becoming.
You are already seen.

And when the time is right, **you won't miss what's meant for you.**

Let's Reflect

1. How are you stewarding your singleness right now?

2. Are there any areas where God is inviting you to heal, grow, or let go?

3. What would it look like to live fully right now—without waiting for a partner?

Prayer

Lord, thank You for this season. Help me to see it as a gift, not a curse. Teach me how to grow, serve, build, and love from a place of wholeness. Prepare my heart for marriage—if that's Your will—but more importantly, prepare my life to glorify You. I trust Your timing. I trust Your way. In Jesus' name, amen.

Affirmation

I am whole in God.
My singleness is not a pause—it's a purpose.
I am preparing in peace, growing in grace, and becoming her now.
I trust God's timing, and I love who I'm becoming.

Final Word

If you made it to this page, I want you to know something: I'm proud of you.

You didn't just read a book—you showed up for yourself. You dared to lean into God's truth about who you are and who you're becoming. You took a sacred step toward the woman He's always seen in you: strong, wise, faithful, and more than rubies.

This journey isn't about perfection. It's about **progress**, one intentional step at a time. Becoming her isn't a final destination—it's a daily decision to choose purpose over pressure, virtue over vanity, and faith over fear.

You'll have days when you feel unstoppable, and days when you feel undone. But even in the in-between, God is working. He's shaping you, stretching you, and smiling over you.

My prayer is that this book has reminded you of your worth, reignited your purpose, and pointed you back to the One who makes all things new. And as you move forward, may you carry this truth in your heart:

You don't have to try to be like her. You already are her.

Keep showing up.
Keep loving deeply.
Keep building boldly.
Keep becoming.

The world needs the woman you are— and the woman you're still becoming.

You are more than rubies.
And you always will be.

With love and faith,

Daphne Nicole Mace

Made in United States
Cleveland, OH
24 May 2025

17180930R00050